# paddle board log book

date:

weather:

time:

location:

distance paddled:

companions:

wow moments:

notes:

date:

weather:

time:

location:

distance paddled:

companions:

wow moments:

notes:

**date:**

**weather:**

**time:**

**location:**

**distance paddled:**

**companions:**

**wow moments:**

**notes:**

date:

weather:

time:

location:

distance paddled:

companions:

wow moments:

notes:

date:

weather:

time:

location:

distance paddled:

companions:

wow moments:

notes:

date:

weather:

time:

location:

distance paddled:

companions:

wow moments:

notes:

date:

weather:

time:

location:

distance paddled:

companions:

wow moments:

notes:

date:

weather:

time:

location:

distance paddled:

companions:

wow moments:

notes:

date:

weather:

time:

location:

distance paddled:

companions:

wow moments:

notes:

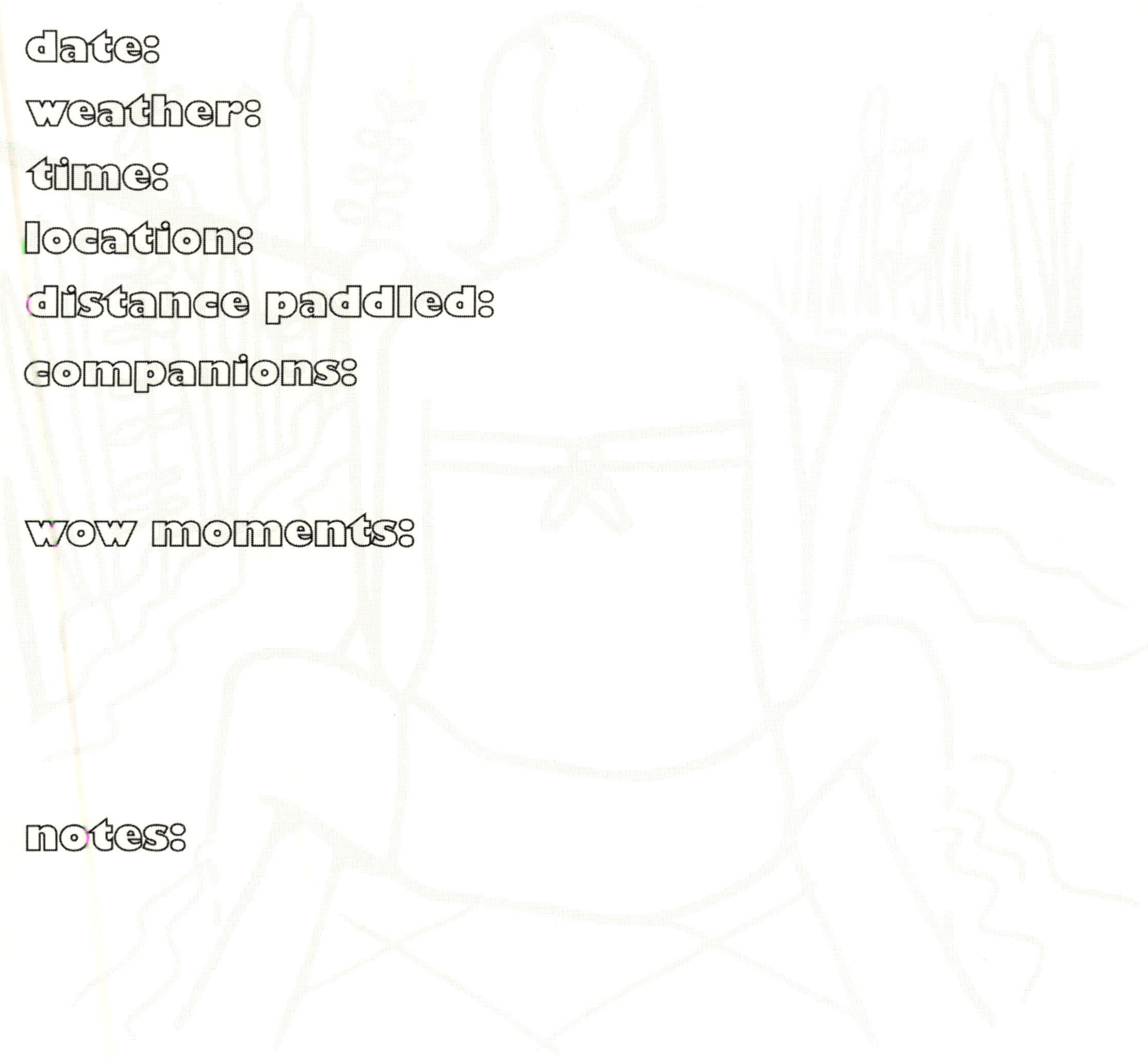

date:

weather:

time:

location:

distance paddled:

companions:

wow moments:

notes:

date:

weather:

time:

location:

distance paddled:

companions:

wow moments:

notes:

date:

weather:

time:

location:

distance paddled:

companions:

wow moments:

notes:

date:

weather:

time:

location:

distance paddled:

companions:

wow moments:

notes:

date:

weather:

time:

location:

distance paddled:

companions:

wow moments:

notes:

date:

weather:

time:

location:

distance paddled:

companions:

wow moments:

notes:

date:

weather:

time:

location:

distance paddled:

companions:

wow moments:

notes:

date:

weather:

time:

location:

distance paddled:

companions:

wow moments:

notes:

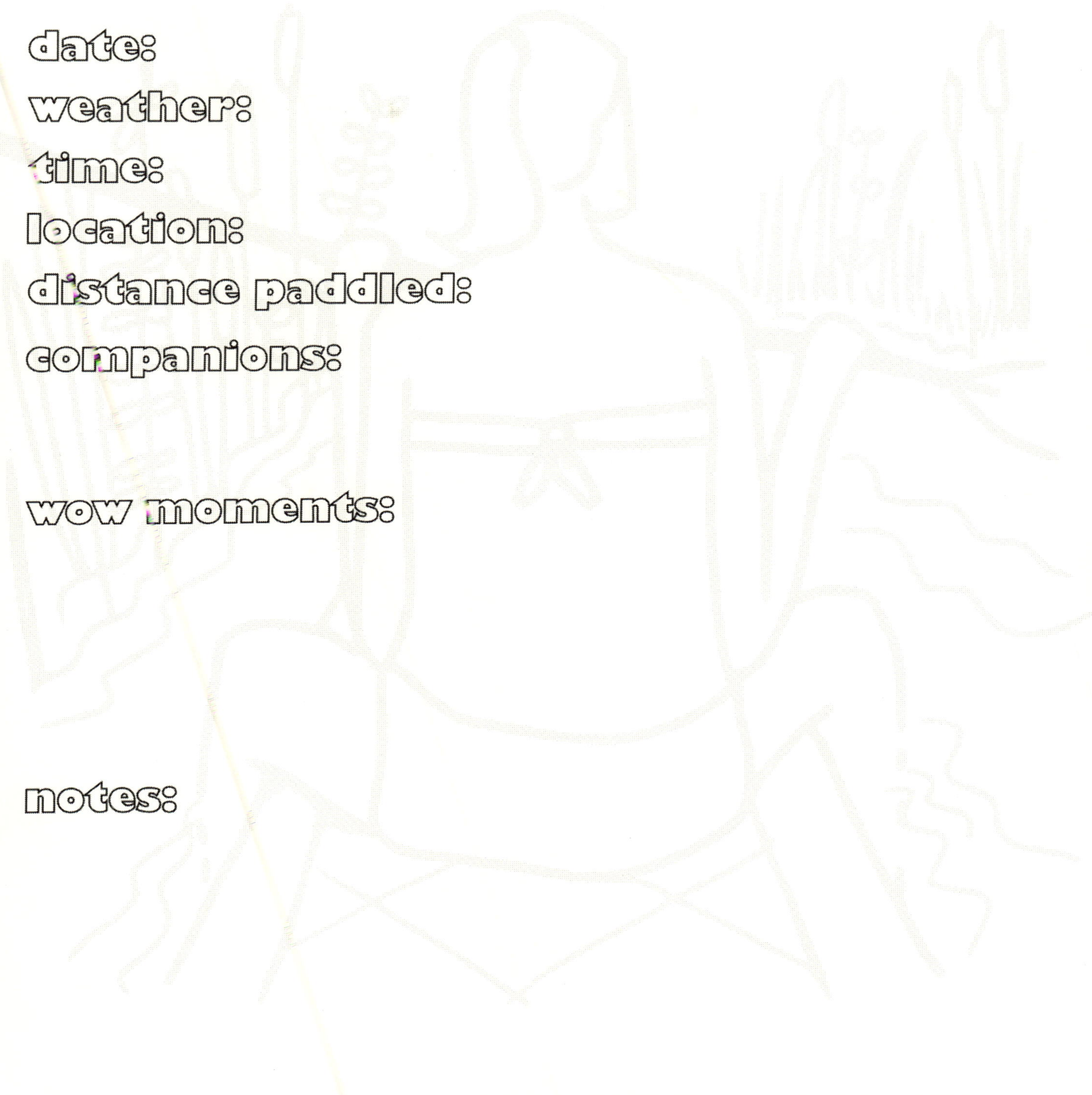

date:

weather:

time:

location:

distance paddled:

companions:

wow moments:

notes:

date:

weather:

time:

location:

distance paddled:

companions:

wow moments:

notes:

date:

weather:

time:

location:

distance paddled:

companions:

wow moments:

notes:

**date:**

**weather:**

**time:**

**location:**

**distance paddled:**

**companions:**

**wow moments:**

**notes:**

date:

weather:

time:

location:

distance paddled:

companions:

wow moments:

notes:

## date:

## weather:

## time:

## location:

## distance paddled:

## companions:

## wow moments:

## notes:

date:

weather:

time:

location:

distance paddled:

companions:

wow moments:

notes:

date:

weather:

time:

location:

distance paddled:

companions:

wow moments:

notes:

date:

weather:

time:

location:

distance paddled:

companions:

wow moments:

notes:

date:

weather:

time:

location:

distance paddled:

companions:

wow moments:

notes:

date:

weather:

time:

location:

distance paddled:

companions:

wow moments:

notes:

**date:**

**weather:**

**time:**

**location:**

**distance paddled:**

**companions:**

**wow moments:**

**notes:**

date:

weather:

time:

location:

distance paddled:

companions:

wow moments:

notes:

date:

weather:

time:

location:

distance paddled:

companions:

wow moments:

notes:

date:

weather:

time:

location:

distance paddled:

companions:

wow moments:

notes:

date:

weather:

time:

location:

distance paddled:

companions:

wow moments:

notes:

date:

weather:

time:

location:

distance paddled:

companions:

wow moments:

notes:

date:

weather:

time:

location:

distance paddled:

companions:

wow moments:

notes:

date:

weather:

time:

location:

distance paddled:

companions:

wow moments:

notes:

date:

weather:

time:

location:

distance paddled:

companions:

wow moments:

notes:

date:

weather:

time:

location:

distance paddled:

companions:

wow moments:

notes:

date:

weather:

time:

location:

distance paddled:

companions:

wow moments:

notes:

date:

weather:

time:

location:

distance paddled:

companions:

wow moments:

notes:

date:

weather:

time:

location:

distance paddled:

companions:

wow moments:

notes:

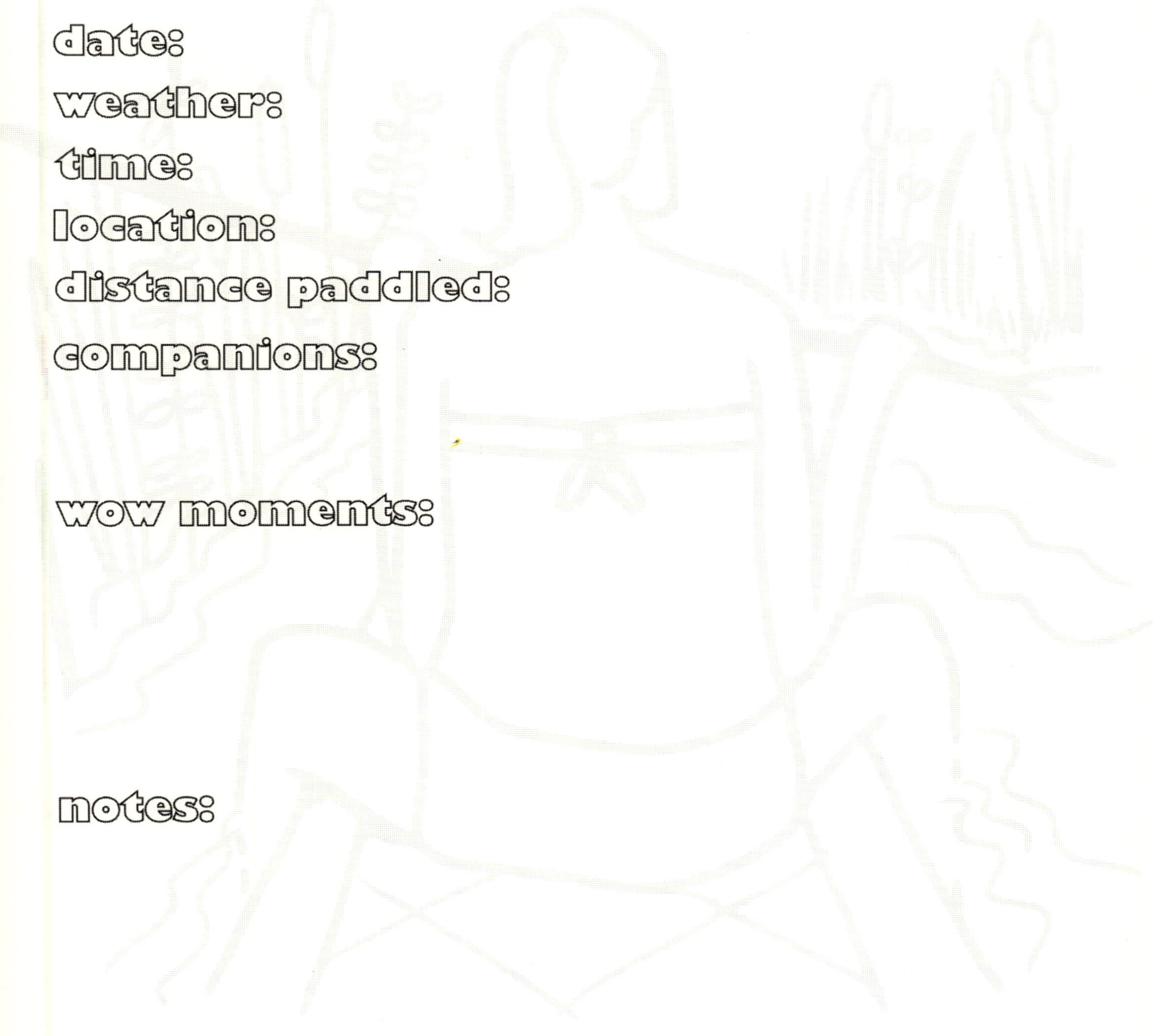

date:

weather:

time:

location:

distance paddled:

companions:

wow moments:

notes:

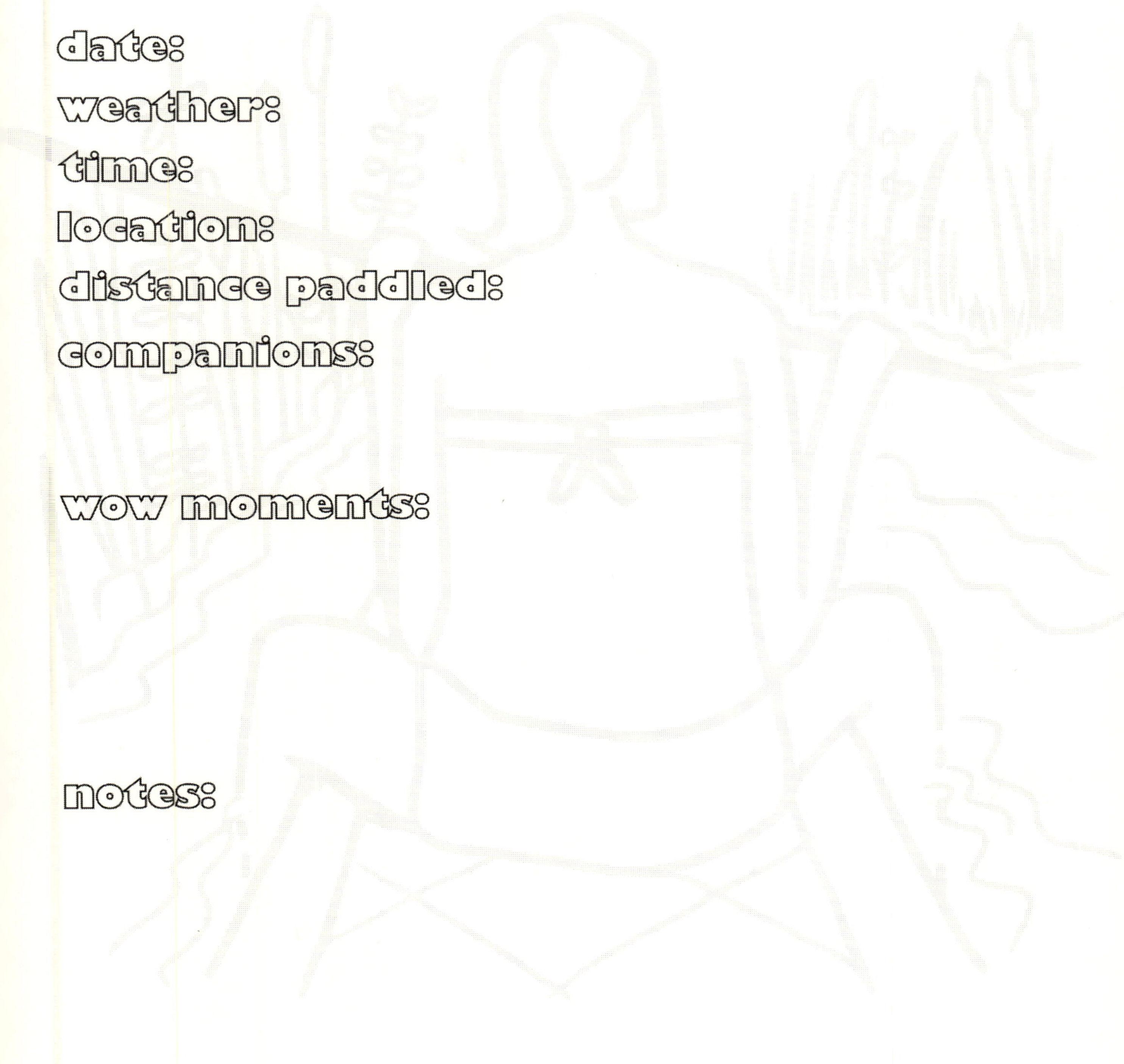

date:

weather:

time:

location:

distance paddled:

companions:

wow moments:

notes:

date:

weather:

time:

location:

distance paddled:

companions:

wow moments:

notes:

date:

weather:

time:

location:

distance paddled:

companions:

wow moments:

notes:

date:

weather:

time:

location:

distance paddled:

companions:

wow moments:

notes:

**date:**

**weather:**

**time:**

**location:**

**distance paddled:**

**companions:**

**wow moments:**

**notes:**

date:

weather:

time:

location:

distance paddled:

companions:

wow moments:

notes:

date:

weather:

time:

location:

distance paddled:

companions:

wow moments:

notes:

date:

weather:

time:

location:

distance paddled:

companions:

wow moments:

notes:

date:

weather:

time:

location:

distance paddled:

companions:

wow moments:

notes:

date:

weather:

time:

location:

distance paddled:

companions:

wow moments:

notes:

date:

weather:

time:

location:

distance paddled:

companions:

wow moments:

notes:

date:

weather:

time:

location:

distance paddled:

companions:

wow moments:

notes:

date:

weather:

time:

location:

distance paddled:

companions:

wow moments:

notes:

date:

weather:

time:

location:

distance paddled:

companions:

wow moments:

notes:

date:

weather:

time:

location:

distance paddled:

companions:

wow moments:

notes:

date:

weather:

time:

location:

distance paddled:

companions:

wow moments:

notes:

date:

weather:

time:

location:

distance paddled:

companions:

wow moments:

notes:

**date:**

**weather:**

**time:**

**location:**

**distance paddled:**

**companions:**

**wow moments:**

**notes:**

date:

weather:

time:

location:

distance paddled:

companions:

wow moments:

notes:

date:

weather:

time:

location:

distance paddled:

companions:

wow moments:

notes:

date:

weather:

time:

location:

distance paddled:

companions:

wow moments:

notes:

date:

weather:

time:

location:

distance paddled:

companions:

wow moments:

notes:

date:

weather:

time:

location:

distance paddled:

companions:

wow moments:

notes:

date:

weather:

time:

location:

distance paddled:

companions:

wow moments:

notes:

date:

weather:

time:

location:

distance paddled:

companions:

wow moments:

notes:

date:

weather:

time:

location:

distance paddled:

companions:

wow moments:

notes:

date:

weather:

time:

location:

distance paddled:

companions:

wow moments:

notes:

date:

weather:

time:

location:

distance paddled:

companions:

wow moments:

notes:

date:

weather:

time:

location:

distance paddled:

companions:

wow moments:

notes:

date:

weather:

time:

location:

distance paddled:

companions:

wow moments:

notes:

date:

weather:

time:

location:

distance paddled:

companions:

wow moments:

notes:

date:

weather:

time:

location:

distance paddled:

companions:

wow moments:

notes:

date:

weather:

time:

location:

distance paddled:

companions:

wow moments:

notes:

date:

weather:

time:

location:

distance paddled:

companions:

wow moments:

notes:

date:

weather:

time:

location:

distance paddled:

companions:

wow moments:

notes:

date:

weather:

time:

location:

distance paddled:

companions:

wow moments:

notes:

date:

weather:

time:

location:

distance paddled:

companions:

wow moments:

notes:

date:

weather:

time:

location:

distance paddled:

companions:

wow moments:

notes:

**date:**

**weather:**

**time:**

**location:**

**distance paddled:**

**companions:**

**wow moments:**

**notes:**

date:

weather:

time:

location:

distance paddled:

companions:

wow moments:

notes:

date:

weather:

time:

location:

distance paddled:

companions:

wow moments:

notes:

date:

weather:

time:

location:

distance paddled:

companions:

wow moments:

notes:

date:

weather:

time:

location:

distance paddled:

companions:

wow moments:

notes:

date:

weather:

time:

location:

distance paddled:

companions:

wow moments:

notes:

**date:**

**weather:**

**time:**

**location:**

**distance paddled:**

**companions:**

**wow moments:**

**notes:**

date:

weather:

time:

location:

distance paddled:

companions:

wow moments:

notes:

**date:**

**weather:**

**time:**

**location:**

**distance paddled:**

**companions:**

**wow moments:**

**notes:**

date:

weather:

time:

location:

distance paddled:

companions:

wow moments:

notes:

date:

weather:

time:

location:

distance paddled:

companions:

wow moments:

notes:

date:

weather:

time:

location:

distance paddled:

companions:

wow moments:

notes:

date:

weather:

time:

location:

distance paddled:

companions:

wow moments:

notes:

date:

weather:

time:

location:

distance paddled:

companions:

wow moments:

notes:

date:

weather:

time:

location:

distance paddled:

companions:

wow moments:

notes:

date:

weather:

time:

location:

distance paddled:

companions:

wow moments:

notes:

date:

weather:

time:

location:

distance paddled:

companions:

wow moments:

notes:

date:

weather:

time:

location:

distance paddled:

companions:

wow moments:

notes:

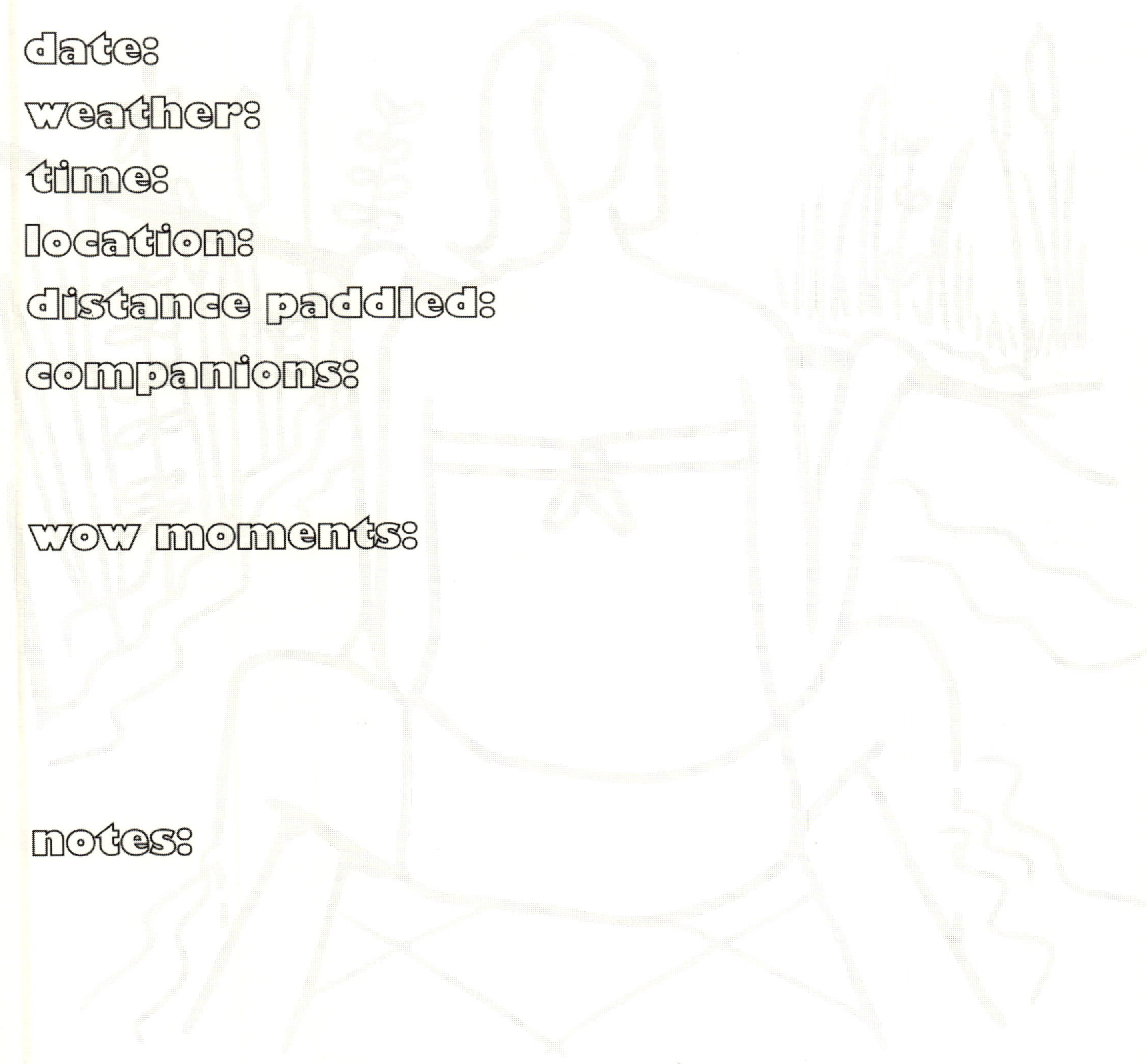

date:

weather:

time:

location:

distance paddled:

companions:

wow moments:

notes:

date:

weather:

time:

location:

distance paddled:

companions:

wow moments:

notes:

date:

weather:

time:

location:

distance paddled:

companions:

wow moments:

notes:

date:

weather:

time:

location:

distance paddled:

companions:

wow moments:

notes:

date:

weather:

time:

location:

distance paddled:

companions:

wow moments:

notes:

date:

weather:

time:

location:

distance paddled:

companions:

wow moments:

notes:

date:

weather:

time:

location:

distance paddled:

companions:

wow moments:

notes:

date:

weather:

time:

location:

distance paddled:

companions:

wow moments:

notes:

date:

weather:

time:

location:

distance paddled:

companions:

wow moments:

notes:

**date:**

**weather:**

**time:**

**location:**

**distance paddled:**

**companions:**

**wow moments:**

**notes:**

date:

weather:

time:

location:

distance paddled:

companions:

wow moments:

notes:

date:

weather:

time:

location:

distance paddled:

companions:

wow moments:

notes:

**date:**

**weather:**

**time:**

**location:**

**distance paddled:**

**companions:**

**wow moments:**

**notes:**

date:

weather:

time:

location:

distance paddled:

companions:

wow moments:

notes:

date:

weather:

time:

location:

distance paddled:

companions:

wow moments:

notes:

date:

weather:

time:

location:

distance paddled:

companions:

wow moments:

notes:

date:

weather:

time:

location:

distance paddled:

companions:

wow moments:

notes:

date:

weather:

time:

location:

distance paddled:

companions:

wow moments:

notes:

**date:**

**weather:**

**time:**

**location:**

**distance paddled:**

**companions:**

**wow moments:**

**notes:**

date:

weather:

time:

location:

distance paddled:

companions:

wow moments:

notes:

date:

weather:

time:

location:

distance paddled:

companions:

wow moments:

notes:

date:

weather:

time:

location:

distance paddled:

companions:

wow moments:

notes:

date:

weather:

time:

location:

distance paddled:

companions:

wow moments:

notes:

date:

weather:

time:

location:

distance paddled:

companions:

wow moments:

notes:

date:

weather:

time:

location:

distance paddled:

companions:

wow moments:

notes:

date:

weather:

time:

location:

distance paddled:

companions:

wow moments:

notes:

date:

weather:

time:

location:

distance paddled:

companions:

wow moments:

notes:

date:

weather:

time:

location:

distance paddled:

companions:

wow moments:

notes:

date:

weather:

time:

location:

distance paddled:

companions:

wow moments:

notes:

date:

weather:

time:

location:

distance paddled:

companions:

wow moments:

notes:

**date:**

**weather:**

**time:**

**location:**

**distance paddled:**

**companions:**

**wow moments:**

**notes:**

date:

weather:

time:

location:

distance paddled:

companions:

wow moments:

notes:

date:

weather:

time:

location:

distance paddled:

companions:

wow moments:

notes:

date:

weather:

time:

location:

distance paddled:

companions:

wow moments:

notes:

date:

weather:

time:

location:

distance paddled:

companions:

wow moments:

notes:

date:

weather:

time:

location:

distance paddled:

companions:

wow moments:

notes:

date:

weather:

time:

location:

distance paddled:

companions:

wow moments:

notes:

date:

weather:

time:

location:

distance paddled:

companions:

wow moments:

notes:

date:

weather:

time:

location:

distance paddled:

companions:

wow moments:

notes:

date:

weather:

time:

location:

distance paddled:

companions:

wow moments:

notes:

date:

weather:

time:

location:

distance paddled:

companions:

wow moments:

notes:

date:

weather:

time:

location:

distance paddled:

companions:

wow moments:

notes:

date:

weather:

time:

location:

distance paddled:

companions:

wow moments:

notes:

date:

weather:

time:

location:

distance paddled:

companions:

wow moments:

notes:

date:

weather:

time:

location:

distance paddled:

companions:

wow moments:

notes:

date:

weather:

time:

location:

distance paddled:

companions:

wow moments:

notes:

date:

weather:

time:

location:

distance paddled:

companions:

wow moments:

notes:

date:

weather:

time:

location:

distance paddled:

companions:

wow moments:

notes:

date:

weather:

time:

location:

distance paddled:

companions:

wow moments:

notes:

date:

weather:

time:

location:

distance paddled:

companions:

wow moments:

notes:

date:

weather:

time:

location:

distance paddled:

companions:

wow moments:

notes:

date:

weather:

time:

location:

distance paddled:

companions:

wow moments:

notes:

date:

weather:

time:

location:

distance paddled:

companions:

wow moments:

notes:

date:

weather:

time:

location:

distance paddled:

companions:

wow moments:

notes:

date:

weather:

time:

location:

distance paddled:

companions:

wow moments:

notes:

**date:**

**weather:**

**time:**

**location:**

**distance paddled:**

**companions:**

**wow moments:**

**notes:**

date:

weather:

time:

location:

distance paddled:

companions:

wow moments:

notes:

date:

weather:

time:

location:

distance paddled:

companions:

wow moments:

notes:

date:

weather:

time:

location:

distance paddled:

companions:

wow moments:

notes:

date:

weather:

time:

location:

distance paddled:

companions:

wow moments:

notes:

date:

weather:

time:

location:

distance paddled:

companions:

wow moments:

notes:

date:

weather:

time:

location:

distance paddled:

companions:

wow moments:

notes:

date:

weather:

time:

location:

distance paddled:

companions:

wow moments:

notes:

date:

weather:

time:

location:

distance paddled:

companions:

wow moments:

notes:

date:

weather:

time:

location:

distance paddled:

companions:

wow moments:

notes:

date:

weather:

time:

location:

distance paddled:

companions:

wow moments:

notes:

date:

weather:

time:

location:

distance paddled:

companions:

wow moments:

notes:

date:

weather:

time:

location:

distance paddled:

companions:

wow moments:

notes:

date:

weather:

time:

location:

distance paddled:

companions:

wow moments:

notes:

date:

weather:

time:

location:

distance paddled:

companions:

wow moments:

notes:

date:

weather:

time:

location:

distance paddled:

companions:

wow moments:

notes:

date:

weather:

time:

location:

distance paddled:

companions:

wow moments:

notes:

date:

weather:

time:

location:

distance paddled:

companions:

wow moments:

notes:

date:

weather:

time:

location:

distance paddled:

companions:

wow moments:

notes:

date:

weather:

time:

location:

distance paddled:

companions:

wow moments:

notes:

date:

weather:

time:

location:

distance paddled:

companions:

wow moments:

notes:

date:

weather:

time:

location:

distance paddled:

companions:

wow moments:

notes:

date:

weather:

time:

location:

distance paddled:

companions:

wow moments:

notes:

date:

weather:

time:

location:

distance paddled:

companions:

wow moments:

notes:

date:

weather:

time:

location:

distance paddled:

companions:

wow moments:

notes:

date:

weather:

time:

location:

distance paddled:

companions:

wow moments:

notes:

date:

weather:

time:

location:

distance paddled:

companions:

wow moments:

notes:

date:

weather:

time:

location:

distance paddled:

companions:

wow moments:

notes:

date:

weather:

time:

location:

distance paddled:

companions:

wow moments:

notes:

**date:**

**weather:**

**time:**

**location:**

**distance paddled:**

**companions:**

**wow moments:**

**notes:**

date:

weather:

time:

location:

distance paddled:

companions:

wow moments:

notes:

date:

weather:

time:

location:

distance paddled:

companions:

wow moments:

notes:

date:

weather:

time:

location:

distance paddled:

companions:

wow moments:

notes:

date:

weather:

time:

location:

distance paddled:

companions:

wow moments:

notes:

date:

weather:

time:

location:

distance paddled:

companions:

wow moments:

notes:

date:

weather:

time:

location:

distance paddled:

companions:

wow moments:

notes:

date:

weather:

time:

location:

distance paddled:

companions:

wow moments:

notes:

date:

weather:

time:

location:

distance paddled:

companions:

wow moments:

notes:

date:

weather:

time:

location:

distance paddled:

companions:

wow moments:

notes:

date:

weather:

time:

location:

distance paddled:

companions:

wow moments:

notes:

date:

weather:

time:

location:

distance paddled:

companions:

wow moments:

notes:

date:

weather:

time:

location:

distance paddled:

companions:

wow moments:

notes:

date:

weather:

time:

location:

distance paddled:

companions:

wow moments:

notes:

date:

weather:

time:

location:

distance paddled:

companions:

wow moments:

notes:

date:

weather:

time:

location:

distance paddled:

companions:

wow moments:

notes:

date:

weather:

time:

location:

distance paddled:

companions:

wow moments:

notes:

date:

weather:

time:

location:

distance paddled:

companions:

wow moments:

notes:

date:

weather:

time:

location:

distance paddled:

companions:

wow moments:

notes:

Manufactured by Amazon.ca
Bolton, ON

31265361R00118